The
Holy
Place

The *Holy* Place

Thoughts from the Pew, After
Thoughts, Thanatos, and The Holy
Place now all in one book. A
collection of poems on life, death,
and the Christian walk.

Paul "Herb" Frazier

Xulon Press

Xulon Press
2301 Lucien Way #415
Maitland, FL 32751
407.339.4217
www.xulonpress.com

Drawings by Paul H. Frazier
Cover design by Alexandria Grace Dotten
Back cover photo by Joel Eden

Printed in the United States of America.

ISBN-13: 978-1-6305-0981-1

Dedication

"But soft, what light through yonder window breaks?
It is the east and " Judith Ann " is the sun."

Forgive me Shakespeare that I use one of my favorite lines from Romeo and Juliet to honor my wife, Judy, who with the God we both love, has always been my main support.

To my daughters and their husbands who have always been positive encouragement and to my grandchildren, a testimony to that which is passed from generation to generation: a love and commitment to YHWH, the King and Creator of all.

Paul "Herb" Frazier

Table of Contents

Thanatos (Death) 39

Thoughts From The Pew

Heykal

BOOK IV

Hebrew: "the holy place" Ex 26:33

"But God chose the foolish things of the world to shame the wise."

1 Corinthians 1:27

Introduction to Book IV

W hy would I start with Book IV when the natural sequence should begin with Book I? I believe that my writings convey a progression of spiritual growth. The contents of Book IV the Lord gave me as He did all my work. Written from 2015-2019, it shows the most recent of a growing relationship with Him.

However, you may begin, if you prefer a more structured approach, with Book I or for that matter at any point for there is no ordered sequence.

Books I, II, and III were previously self-published, but I chose to include them here since the sequence illustrates my personal growth.

I thank God for the words He has given me and I pray that they may draw you closer to Him.

Soli deo gloria

Come

Come with me to the house of our God
That we might give thanks to Him for
All the blessings of His creations
Which He has given unto us.

We lift up our hands in holy praise
To our Father who has come to live with us.
It is our Thanksgiving everyday
For the gift of His Son and Spirit
That lives within us.

All honor, glory and power
Be unto Him who draws us
And all His creation back to Himself.

All praise and thanks
Be to God our Father
Who was and is and is to come.

Come quickly, Lord Jesus.

Cleansing The Temple
2Chron 29:3-ff

Open the doors and repair them.
Carry out the rubbish from the Holy Place.
Cleanse the house of the LORD.
Bring out the debris from the inner part.
Sanctify the house of the LORD.

I am the house of GOD,
The Holy Place where He resides.

A Walk Alone

Alone in the wilderness,
My only company – the Spirit,
And my thoughts.

Gone are the chaos and confusion
That constantly drives away my peace.
I dwell in the shade of righteousness.
Alone, but never alone.

A walk on the wild side
Bemoans the truth
Of the things I've done
When I was a youth.

All have a story,
Few of delight.
Most come from the darkness;
The darkness of night.

A clanging gong
A sounding bell.
All other stories
An announcement from hell.

Rarely a tale
Of peace and of love,
Except for the gift
That came from above.

In the Wilderness

Alone in the wilderness there is a spiritual unification between the Creator and His creation.

Where is this wilderness? It is not necessarily a place, but a being, an attitude, surrounded by grace, immersed in His love and abiding in Him.

I can find this alone on a mountain trail, floating on a hidden lake or in a crowded mall. He is there and He fills my soul with His spirit and calls to me to be His – totally.

Jesus, fill me and quicken me.

What is my daemon?
It haunts me.
It taunts me.
It tries to consume
And I cannot stuff it.
Bury it, deny it.
I dare not try it.
Like love it will take me
And break me.

An explosion within controls what I write,
Controls what I paint to say what I ain't.

A Wilderness Trek

I was with Him
On a wilderness trek.
The baggage of my past
Hung 'round my neck.

My bullied past
Brought naught but strife,
But in this moment
I found life.

He came to me
From up above
And filled my heart
With peace and love.

He came to me
And took my sin
And stayed to fight
The war within.

Who Am I?

Remove the façade and what do you see?
Would you say that's really me?
What are you hiding under there?
There are things I don't want to share.
I'm afraid you'll laugh at me
If I uncover for all to see.
As Jean ValJean cried "Who am I?"
What's my life? Am I living a lie?

Where's my example? Where's my mentor?
Unbelieving peers and greater tormentors.
I can't remember pleasant times with my dad.
I can't remember any good times we had.
When I needed him he wasn't there.
I'm so sure he didn't care.
Was it my fault – so far apart?
What did he do to damage my heart?
I needed a father to show me the way,
How I should grow and live each day.

Put away childishness and become a man.
Follow the Spirit as best as I can.
The Spirit will lead me and show me the way.
How I should grow and live each day.
Forgetting the past and all I have done,
The Spirit will lead me to follow the One

continued

Who came to save me and forgive my sin

That I might learn to abide in Him.
God in heaven hear my prayer,
In my need You have always been there.

Cabul

1 Kings 9:13 "Good for Nothing"

"Cabul, Cabul," they said to me.
"Good for nothing you'll always be."
'Twas a lie, but I believed.
Caused a life which I have grieved.
Down in the depths of deathly despair
Not knowing who, what, when or where.

Who is it hides behind the tree?
Is it Adam or is it me?
I've followed him since I was born
Not knowing that I'd draw His scorn.
I have things hidden, even I don't know.
A bully past that I won't show.
He threatens me where'er I turn.
And laughs at me, wants me to burn.
How do I fight it? I don't know.
How do I fight it? Just let it go?

Merciful Lord do they really see
Your blessed love bestowed on me?
Praise Him who created heaven and earth.
In Him I found a new birth.
My life a mess.
My sin I confess.

He has given me new worth.
Come forth oh sin and show your face.
That I might know the depth of grace.

Satan says my life's a waste.
Jesus says "Wake up and taste
The feast that I've prepared for you."
Those days are gone, taken away.
Those days are gone, but want to stay
And bully me the rest of the way.
He stopped the bully in his path.
Crushed his head with His wrath.
Eternally free with hope in my heart.
Eternally free. I have a new start.

When I'm Gone

Don't worry 'bout me
When I'm gone.
All our memories
Will linger on.

I'll be with the Lord,
Singing a new song.
Don't worry 'bout me
When I'm gone.

Tho' I be gone,
Don't worry 'bout me.
I walk with Jesus.
I've been set free.

The heart of all men
Fear death alone.
I have no fear,
I'm going home.

Into His arms
Is where I'll stay.
I'll live for Him
Until that day
When He comes
To take me away.
HALLELU YAH!

Do You Know? Do You Care?

Death is with us everywhere.
Do you know? Do you care?
Read the papers or news on the air.
Do you know? Do you care?

Here I sit and read the paper,
The words before me meaningless vapor.
Twisted tales of sinful man
Exposing lies that say, "I can."

I wish that you were my brother.
I tell you that there is no other
Except He who came to remove our sin
And take us home to be with Him.

After all we've said and done
There is no way except by One
Who gave Himself to take our sin
And bring us home to be with Him.

Open your ears that you might hear!
Open your eyes that you might see!
Open your mind to know the Truth!
Open your heart that you might be
One with Him — Eternally!

Do you know? Do you care?
He is with us everywhere!

Come Up Here

LORD, if I may be so bold,
Even tho' I'm getting old.
I need to know just what to do.
So in my life I'll honor You.

LORD, I will try to run the race
Of life, and then to find my place
Amongst the saints who follow You.
Just tell me LORD, what I must do.

I walk with the saints, tho' far in the rear.
Those in the lead I know could see clear.
I asked, "Where is it we go today?"
And then I heard my Savior say,

"Come up here and walk with me.
Open your eyes and you will see
The path is straight, tho' narrow be.
Leads to your home prepared for thee."

LORD, is there more for me to do
While here on earth I follow You?
"Share my Word and show the others
How to be our loving brothers."

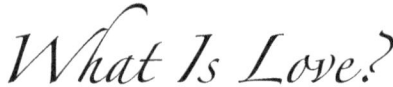

What Is Love?

Repentance-Forgiveness-Redemption

Regardless of what we have done, He welcomes us home to be with Him — Forever.

The Father shows His love for us through the gift of His Son for our forgiveness and redemption.

Maranatha

That which is,
Yet cannot be.
'Less like the blind,
We too can see.
We lift Him up,
Nailed to the tree.
So all who come
Can be set free.
Prevenient grace
Has called to me
And now I come
To be with He
Who was, and is,
Will always be.
My God, my God,
I do love thee.
I pray, dear Lord
To come quickly.

Lost

Lost in a world
Of chaos and sin.
Lost in a world
That beckons me in.
I sense the Spirit
Has moved within.
From worthless confusion
I cried out to Him.
He came, I saw,
No longer dim
My future hope.
I'm born again.

Praise to Yahweh.
Praise Him on high.
Praise you Father.
That is my cry

No Greater Love

I feel the whip
T'was meant for me.
The blood You shed
To set me free.

My sin You took
Upon the cross
That I might live,
-Not suffer loss.

You gave Your life
That I might live.
No greater love
Can any give.

With nail scarred hands
You lift me up
That I'll not have
To bear Your cup.

A crown of thorns
For me You bled
A crown You place
Upon my head.

I cast it down,
Fall at Your feet.
I praise You LORD
For when we meet.

The Gift

He gave me a gift.
One I must use.
One that requires
Things I wouldn't choose.
But the choices are His,
To lead and provide.
I only follow
His Spirit inside.

Lord, reach into me
And feel my need.
Reach into me
And remove my greed.
Plant in me
A spiritual seed.
Lord, reach into me
And fill my need.

Nobody Came

I snuck in a side door
And sat in a pew.
Nobody came and
Asked, "How do you do?"
Nobody said, "Come,
Sit with us here.
Come sit up front
To see and to hear."
Everyone laughing and
Hugging their own.
They left me sitting
Here all alone.
They were talking of sports,
Of hunting and game.
Nobody asked to find
Out why I came.
I thought I could find
Some comfort in here,
But even the words
From the pulpit weren't clear.
He spoke of success,
How prosperity came.
I've tried it all, but
Life was the same.
When the plate came by
I had nothing to give

continued

Except for the sin and
The dirt which I live.
I live a life of
Darkness and gloom.
Where is the light
From the empty tomb?

Truth

Alone in the dark I lay in my bed.
Scary thoughts go 'round my head.
Things that frighten me, things I dread.
How can I get to sleep instead?

I toss and turn, fearing I'll burn.
Knowing I'll get just what I earn.

I sit in front of a garbage dump
And write of what I see.
Debauchery and sin and greed;
I want it all for me.

I did it all. 'Twas vanity.
Grasping for wind, but never free.
I read of the place that I will be;
God's wrath to suffer eternally.

I would, I would, if I knew I could.
I really don't know which way to go.
To the left, to the right, I wrestle all night.
But nothing has changed come morning's first light.

I lied, I cried and then I died.
Even knowing where I was going.
If there's a hell, I'll be there,
Just because I didn't share
The truth I knew, but didn't care.

continued

The world is racing on it's sinful path.
Not ever facing the fact of God's wrath.
Never acknowledging that He is there.
In their evil pursuits, they don't even care.

Why I say "they?" I don't even know.
For I've been a part of their evil show.
'Twas lust and greed that I was driven.
Not seeing the truth that I'm forgiven.

The accuser points a finger at me.
I fall to my knees in guilt and shame.
My Savior comes and lifts me up
And takes my sin and all my blame.
It's strength I want; it's strength I need.
Strength to help me do each deed.
Strength that only You can give.
Strength to help me truly live.

Lord, help me to see how you set me free.
Hung on that tree, You died for me.
A sinful man, though I try not to be.
I can't hide my sin, my depravity.

Truth has risen from the dead.
Driven by love to die in my stead.
Son of God, He is the head
Of the body, Spirit led.

3D

The deep darkness of depression
Discovered in the depths of depravity
Wherein I lust and lie
Doubting His Word, I decry.
Here in solitude the mystery
Of Salvation gained before I die.
Frustration is not what I want to live for,
But it seems to be always at the door.
Do this, do that – I don't have the time,
But I'm always waiting in somebody's line.
There is a mountain set before me.
It's locale by reason find.
But in it's darkness, clouds and mist;
Only faith can help me climb.
Sinai calls, I want to answer,
Fear and trembling hinders me.
Hold me Lord, guiding, leading.
In your hands I place my trust.
Climb with me, if I must.
"Flee as a bird unto your mountain." {Ps11:1}
Where is my mountain?
I search for the way.
I know in my soul
That I cannot stay.
But climb I must

continued

For death comes my way.
Whence come the clouds
Of darkness and fear?
I only know that
He is here.
The finger of God
Carves on the stone
A message from Him
That we're not alone.

Take Me Home

Take Me Home, Take Me Home.
For I've Lost My Way.
The Things I've Done I Cannot Say.
Take Me Home, I've Lost My Way.

Thoughts And Acts
All Go Astray.
Take Me Home, I've Lost My Way.

Take Me Home, Take Me Home.
Is This The Day To Take Me Home?

Jesus Comes To Take Me Home.
Is This The Day?
I Will Not Roam.

Take Me Home, Take Me Home.
Jesus Come And Take Me Home.

Holy Spirit Fire

There is a bit of pyromaniac in every man.

To feel the flame of love where'er he can.

To stoke the heat of his desire

And melt the heart with burning fire.

He longs to feel the warm embrace

The memory which he can't erase.

Holy Spirit fire fills me with His love.

Holy Spirit fire sent by Jesus from above.

Boredom

Boredom, sheer boredom

Designed to drive one crazy.

My stomach hurts, my brain's gone dead

My eyes are all too hazy.

My speech whispers out of the dust

As those who besiege Ariel.

As a hungry man dreams – and eats,

But he awakes and his soul is still empty. (Isa.29)

Irritation and frustration

Cause heart palpitations.

Their thoughts and their plans

Are wind and confusion.

They are all worthless,

Their works are nothing. (Isa. 41:29)

Frost's Words

Why should I stop to see?

There's nothing there for me.

'Cept burned up bark

and scraggled limbs.

A life that's wasted,

Not meant to be.

What is this that I must see?

A longed for love?

A most certainty?

Rotten fruit and

Dried up root?

Dealt a blow too hard to feel,

Will last for all eternity.

Abide, Abide

Dark is the night before the dawn

The fog moves in and lingers on.

My inner soul wherein resides

The Spirit of the living God.

I close my eyes in darkness

And a mist surrounds my head.

While worldly things are cast aside

As I focus on Him instead.

I cannot see nor can I feel,

But only taste His presence is real.

Abide, abide we both shall be

I in Him and He in me.

Totally enjoined as one set free.

Here a clap of mystical thunder

Sounded by God to render asunder

All there is but He and I

Together bound and never die.

Darkness

What is night without vision?
All is darkness without truth.
Evil lurks in each dimension.
I have wasted all my youth.
The law no hindrance,
Lust commands.
Placed it all,
Within my hands.

I hear you Lord, but do not do
All the things you want me to.
You hide your face from us to see.
Cares and riches choking me.
Judgement comes,
We're cast away
In outer darkness
There we'll stay.

Eating flesh from human carcass.
Crunching, smashing, breaking bones.
Boiling babies in a cauldron,
Eating them like tea and scones.
Because of sin your back is turned
You don't hear our cries and moans.
Seeing that which we have burned.
Evil, evil we have churned.

Ignoring You, we have not learned.
We chose pleasure
For our treasure.
And we've sinned without measure
For we chose to chase the whore.
Now He evens up the score.
Death is ours
Forevermore.
Death is ours
Forevermore!

Darkness To Light

In the darkness of prayer
I saw Him there.
Meaningless now everywhere.
The life I lived beyond this chair
Has brought me down beyond despair.
The stuff I had, my former fare
With His love does not compare.

Pain released, suffering gone.
Light replaces Satan's song.
Transcending knowledge,
All other love.
Into the darkness,
The light from above.

Transformed life –
One God, one Love.
One in unison –
ONE.

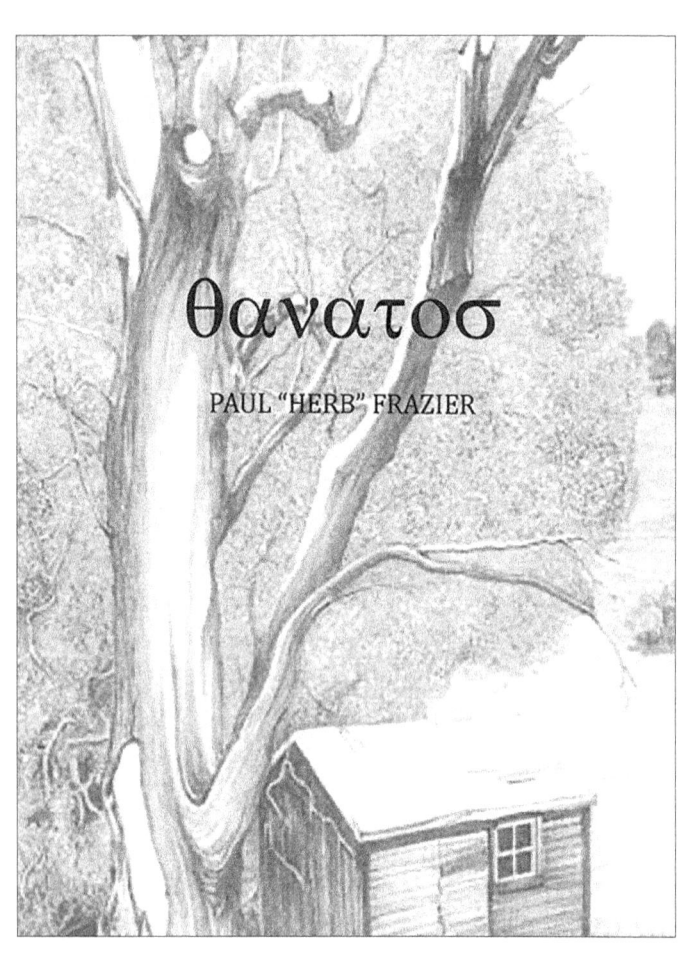

θανατοσ

PAUL "HERB" FRAZIER

Thanatos
(Death)

Book III

"Herb stares down death without flinching because of his faith in the One who rose again. His words are spare and real; they will make you think and feel." Dr. Shane W. Houle (D.Min.)

Director of Scripture Engagement
Bibles For The World

Thanatopsis
A poem giving the author's thoughts about death.

Introduction to Book III

My third book "THANATOS", which is Greek for "DEATH", was motivated by the death of my two brothers, two close friends, and two small children from our church family, all within the previous 12 months.

Some might think it to be a morbid topic, but as especially noted in "Good Friends Dying", it always ends on a high note of optimism and hope.

The cover drawing is of an actual tree I found on CR86, just west of the town of Elizabeth, Colorado. Two weeks after completing the drawing, the tree broke off and only the stump remained. Perhaps some day I'll go back and draw the stump.

The writing "Life and Death" relates not only to the tree, but to me personally.

Soli Deo Gloria

"*Midway upon the journey of our life*
I found myself within a forest dark,
For the straightforward pathway had been lost."

Dante "Inferno"
Canto 1 Lines 1-3

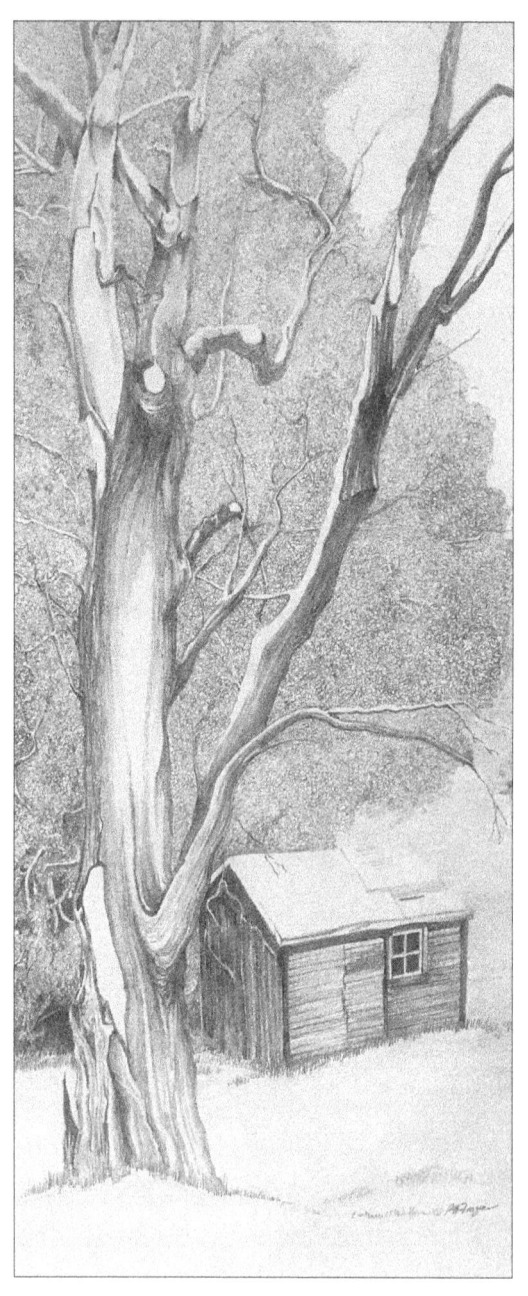

44 / Paul "Herb" Frazier

Life and Death

M any years ago, 60, 70, 80 or more, a small sprout, perhaps with a leaf or two, pushed its way through the crust of the earth. It had already been growing roots where God planted it in good soil. Daily, with the gifts God gave, sun, water, nutrients, it grew. God protected it from animals, weather and man. While still a young plant, it suffered a crisis; an accident, a storm, a disease, a broken limb; and left a scar that it carried throughout its life. A deep scar everyone saw and wondered what had happened. But the young tree overcame that and other difficulties and continued to grow - stronger and bigger - each day. It reached thick and heavy limbs heavenward and spread many branches - a covering, a shelter and a home for many animals and birds that built nests in its thick foliage and under its shade. Winter frost and summer heat only made it grow bigger and stronger.

Then one day its leaves began to fall, not to grow back. Its limbs became weak and some would break off. Soon it stood empty and bare, scarred, wrinkled, and old, awaiting its return to the soil from which it came.

May it enjoy eternal peace. Hallelu YAH!

Thanatopsis

I've been to where the rocking chair

Stops its beat that I might sleep.

I can't remain and fight this slumber,

For God has called my final number.

They found me there slumped o'er my chair.

My lungs would fill no more with air.

"He looks as though he's passed through deep

And lonely places in his sleep."

I count but loss what I have done.

Gained worldly goods and selfish fun.

Oh Lord, that I would meet You there

In far off places in the air.

A place that I would never cry,

For You will dry my tearful eye.

But for His cross I'd be undone,

And now in death we'll be as one.

From The Pit

He came one day

And called to me.

I turned away

And failed to see

The truth was there,

I didn't care.

I wanted things to go my way.

It went my way

And so I burn.

And now I know,

I have discerned.

Nothing gained,

Nothing learned.

In hell I know

It's what I earned.

Die You Demons

Die you demons straight from hell.

I fight you every day.

My armor's old, I'm growing cold

But I still know the Way.

Die you demons of the night.

Thought that you could make me fright.

Though I'm old and growing cold

But I still know the Light.

The battle's His, He comes to fight.

Perhaps He'll take me home tonight.

Good Friends Dying

Good friends dying

Others near death,

In hospice lying,

Taking last breath.

Prayers to recover

Is not what they need.

But a reminder

Of His perfect deed.

To look beyond death.

To see in His rising

A new life for us

Is not so surprising.

His promise is there

That He would come.

There'll be no despair

When He takes us home.

continued

I too shall die

And enter new life.

Forever with Him

To live with no strife.

All stress will be gone,

All tears wiped away.

Eternally sure,

A glorious day.

We'll meet again.

He knows just when

The Spirit will take us

To live there with Him.

A beautiful day

Resplendent with light.

More majestic than mountains.

What a glorious sight.

All glory be to God on high.

In majesty He reigns forever.

HALLELU YAH!

All He Did Was Cross The Street

All he did was cross the street.
Never knowing what fate he would meet.
He looked to the left and he looked to the right,
But didn't see that car that night
That twisted his legs and crushed his chest
Doctors said, "We've done our best
And can't do more. Just lay him to rest."

What do you do when you've lost a son?
Only hope you'll ne'er be the one
To suffer such loss, to suffer such pain.
Could good come from this? Can there be any gain?

God must have cried when His Son died
And Satan laughed thinking he had won.
But God knew what He would do.
Raise Him up for me and for you.

Help me Lord to meet the test.
Help me Lord to do my best.
To follow You and never protest.
To trust and believe that You know best.

Now I Burn

Someone came to lift me up.

I just laughed, a strong rebuff.

They don't know what they say.

I came here just to play.

I don't want to hear their word.

Bunch of noises, all absurd.

Like a pig, I love the mud.

Sinking deeper in the crud.

Life has wrought a cruel turn.

Tried it out and now I burn.

My Flag

My flag slid down the pole.

I don't know why

It's at half mast. Oh my!

Did I die? Not I!

Next time when I walk by

I'll raise it back up high

And tighten tight the tie,

To fly until I die.

On That Day

Not a day goes by that I don't sin.

In my fear I turn to Him

And ask for mercy in my prayer

Expose my sin and show me where

I went wrong and didn't care.

Short on love and long on anger

My acts have put my soul in danger.

Although He loves me, I don't obey.

Will He reject me on that day?

"Not everyone who says unto me 'Lord, Lord' will enter the Kingdom of Heaven, but only he who does the will of my Father who is in Heaven." Mat 7:21

Death and Woes

There is a man of flesh and blood

Who knows not where he goes.

He heard the Word and turned away.

Decided he would rather play.

Flesh leads him down an empty street

And brings him death and woes.

He lives a life of crowded stuff

That pushes truth aside.

He doesn't know that what he craves

Will rust and rot inside.

The wrath of God shall come one day

He will know longer want to play.

Lustful Thoughts

My lustful thoughts o'er powered me.

Your law I did eschew.

Satan stole my heart away.

Time with You I did not do.

How can it be I did not see

Your love for me hung on that tree?

Forgive me Lord my evil past.

To think that I could even fast

And pray and ask for mercy,

Lord, Your love so vast.

I know You came to set me free.

A lowly worm, such as me.

Open my eyes that I might see

All that You have done for me.

A Story Divine

If I were a writer what would I write?

I'd ask the Lord to give me insight.

The thoughts and words that speak of life;

Tales of wonder, tales of strife.

Lines that rhyme (not all the time);

That tell a story of divine

Justice, mercy, grace sublime.

Lord, is there something I don't see?

Give me sight and set me free.

Free to be all I can be.

Free to be a slave to thee.

Free to be a chosen one.

Free to follow the only One

That can take my sin away

And bring me to His arms to stay.

The Mountain

There is a mountain before me.

It once was far away.

But now it is much closer,

Which I must face this day.

Lord, remove this mountain

Or please show me the way

Around, or through, or over.

This is what I pray.

I'll begin the climb, Lord.

I'll not go astray.

As long as You are with me,

Guiding these feet of clay.

Although it's most foreboding,

Anxious I will not be.

With thankful prayer and petition

Your answer I will see.

From The Back Pew

I sit in the pew and criticize the few,

Or the many who do not do as I do.

Help me Lord to see only You.

I point to the speck in my brother's eye,

Not seeing the log in my own.

Why can't they see it's for help I plea?

But instead they leave me alone.

I would remain lost less one show the cost

To the One who would make me His own.

If only they'd care; if only they'd share.

But they point to the seeds they have sown.

Except that the seeds are self-interest weeds

And still I am left all alone.

Because of my sin they won't let me in.

They sing and they pray and all of them say

How much they love one another.

continued

What must I do to join the few

Who refuse to call me their brother?

They don't see my need, tho' they worship their creed.

I'll go in search of another.

Perhaps one will come and show me the way.

Perhaps I can find how to live day to day.

I'm tired of the games these church people play.

I no longer listen to all that they say.

Their lives don't uphold the truths that they've told.

I've wasted my life, now I'm growing old.

I see and I plea, "Have mercy on me."

Not Today

I came and asked Him how I could get through heaven's doors.

He said I must get rid of all the things that He abhors.

My love for all the stuff I have; the things I like to do.

"Get rid of all my things?" I asked, "And then come follow You?

Why can't I bring them with me? I would share them on our way."

He said, "No need for all of that. I'll provide for you each day."

It saddened me to think of getting rid of what I had.

I could tell it sorrowed Him and made Him feel real sad,

That I should choose to keep my stuff and not to follow Him.

I walked away with heavy heart and felt my light go dim.

The Light Tonight

The light tonight is not so bright.

The darkness brings on fear and fright.

I need to keep my Lord in sight

So that my life is His delight

And all I do is pure and right.

That I would love my God above

With all my heart, soul, mind and might.

At The Terminal

The best laid rest because the test

Had yet begun to show

Lest all the world upon its quest

Barely could meet the flow.

Midst mustard seed and watercress

They chose a life of emptiness

Beneath the ice and snow.

Rest assured that life obscured

Will not follow truth.

That which denied cannot hide

Obscenely raised uncouth.

In circles great the people wait

Lined up to travel with their mate.

Simple and proud the crowd is loud

Blind to their approaching date.

At the gate await their fate.

continued

With many a noise they've brought their toys

Expecting eternal play.

They haven't learned and never discerned

That this will be their day.

The most important day of all

When Christ the Judge their name will call.

They did not see, it's up to He

Who died that we might all be free.

Not all listened, not all came.

Many rejected His Holy Name.

This day they'll find eternity

Amidst Gehanna's flame.

Found

Mixed between the sea of green

And brown I saw all turned

Up-side-down while the earth

Went round and round.

I couldn't hear because the sound

Of screaming fear and silent death

Would pound and pound

And sear my ear.

Care I not where I'm bound?

Just a mound on the ground.

Surely I've been found –

– Been found.

My Sin

I fear the judge who knows it all.

I fear the judge who since the fall,

Declared that death must pay for all

The sin that I have wallowed in.

Sins are gone; no longer taunt.

He's taken them from out the haunt

And tossed them farthest to the sea.

They can no longer bother me.

Age

My age is beginning to show.

My movements starting to slow.

The answers I don't always know.

My memory sometimes will go.

But His love I still hope to show.

To others His Spirit will flow.

The light He gave me still glow.

As I walk and I talk here below.

My Salvation

Lord, I can't remember when

A day went by I didn't sin.

Tho' I try to do things right

My flesh demands to blind my sight.

Death for sin is what I owe.

Nothing good for me to show.

He took my sin and bore the pain

That I in Him might also reign.

From death to life to Him I cling.

Praise be to God, this song I sing.

Only God can make me whole.

Only Christ can save my soul.

Going Home

Narrow the gate and straight the path

We must take to avoid God's wrath.

His life He gave that we might have

A place with Him that we call home.

My heart is beating ever fast.

The clock is ticking, time has passed.

I don't know how long I'll last

Until He comes to take me home.

His word commands, obey I must

And on His promises I trust.

Ashes to ashes, dust to dust;

That's when He comes to take me home.

No more sorrows, no more tears,

No more heartaches, no more fears.

Only love through all the years

When He comes to take me home.

continued

I praise you Lord, for that's my cry;

To be with you and never die.

All glory be to God on high.

For I am ready to go home.

To Father, Son and Holy Ghost

I lift my cup and give a toast

To bless His name, He gave the most.

So when He comes He'll take me home.

I'm going home to be with Him;

And leave behind this world of sin.

Out of the dark, Spirit within

Going home to be with Him.

Thanksgiving

DID YOU KNOW?

That in this country,
The wealthiest nation in the world,
That 1 out of every 30 children
Are homeless,
And that 1/3 of them are under
The age of 6?

62% of all homeless are children.
2.5 million children.
Growing 13.2% per year.

I'm so thankful that God
Has blessed me
With 2 houses plus a condo,
2 cars, 2 boats and much more
And that I'm going to give
A turkey on Thanksgiving.

When I stand before God
I can say, "I gave a turkey!"

God have mercy on me!

Dead Roots That Grow

I set to take a stump out.

It didn't want to go.

It sent its roots down deep,

So fast and strong to grow.

It fought and fought to stay alive

Tho' I knew that I would win.

For Christ had cut off all the roots

That caused my life of sin.

With one last strength I pulled it out

And threw it in the fire.

I never thought it'd be so hard

To make the thing expire.

I happened by that selfsame spot

A month or two from then.

And little shoots from once dead roots

Were tempting me again.

Cut them off! Dig them up!

Do not let them grow.

For little shoots make big roots

That drag me down below.

Though I'm dead to sin

With Christ within,

The roots still try to grow.

If I give in and let them win

To hell is where I'll go.

My Brothers

I don't know, best I can tell

Both my brothers are in hell.

I didn't try enough to save

And now I'm headed to my grave.

O God, my God, forgive my sin

Or will I spend all time with them?

Jesus died for all my sin

So I could spend all time with Him.

Out My Window

Out my window there's a tree.

In my window, only me.

Both the same, growing old.

Days are past when we were bold.

Living life through heat and cold.

Broken bough, scarred up bark

Loving light, hating dark.

When he falls where will I be?

Make me, Lord, a sturdy tree.

Considered Choice

All mixed betwixt and 'tween the scene

Obscured by work or washing clean.

Results of toil or duty done,

Then on to play and having fun.

No time to rest, just time to run.

To meet the test and grab the best

As I move from sun to sun.

To make the next event filled day

Better than the former one.

Until exhaustion lays me low

And then I've only time to go.

To where? I know,

But failed to show

Considered choice.

The fatal blow.

The End of Life

Win some, lose some

Varicose veins

Nocturnal cramps

Arthritic pains

Memories lost

Not to regain

Weakened vigor

Nothing to gain

Growing old

Going insane

Burning hot

Riddled and shot

Nothing to lose

But an empty pot.

AFTER THOUGHTS

PAUL "HERB" FRAZIER

Afterthoughts

BOOK II

"Eclectic, engaging and fun. Just when you think you have figured where he is heading, Herb throws a curve, often causing us to lean in closer to the plate called home."

Rev. Raymond W. Cameron, Jr.
First Presbyterian Church (ARP)
Lake Placid, Florida

Try It — You'll Like It

I don't know, but I've been told

"All that glitters is not gold."

It looks good from where I stand.

Sure looks good, sure looks grand.

I'll just try a little bit.

I can't see the harm in it.

Wow, it shines with beauty rare.

I must have some, I don't care.

Are they really that sincere?

Or do they fight it due to fear?

I'll just try a little bit.

I can't see the harm in it.

Spiral downward into dust

Worms and dirt, decay and rust.

And now I know I can't escape

Consequences are my fate.

I'll just try a little bit.

I can't see the harm in it.

My Oldest Granddaughter

She's a beauty. She's divine.

Her spirit always dwells with Thine.

She's the oldest granddaughter of mine.

Truly a jewel of great design.

Her light of Christ will always shine.

It shows, she glows from tip to toes.

Brings joy to all where'er she goes.

Her spirit touches all she knows.

Christ's light in her forever glows.

My Middle Granddaughter

Of three granddaughters

She's in the middle.

Loves to sing.

Laughs at a riddle.

Sings like a bird

Or an angel I've heard.

Loves the Lord.

Lives by His Word.

Joy she brings

Whenever she sings.

Songs she writes,

Tears she brings.

Makes my heart soar

As on angel's wings

My Youngest Granddaughter

I woke up early one morning and

Found her sitting near the bottom of the stair,

Just outside my bedroom door.

I don't know how long she had been there.

No one else was awake yet.

She said she had been waiting for me to get up.

The sun shone through an upper window

Encircling her hair like an angel.

Patiently expecting the one God had assigned

Her to be with this day.

The image frozen in my mind.

On days when I rise early

I open my bedroom door

Expecting, hoping, that she would be there.

Knowing my family is somewhere far away,

I miss them, but their memory is alive

And here, always, in my heart.

The Climate

Frozen dreams

Frosted schemes

Hot to trot

For what is not

It isn't surprising

The temperatures rising

All seems well

Closer to hell

Where To Go?

How do I know where I should go?

Weeds to pull, grass to mow;

Both of which continue to grow.

What to do? Where to go?

Fast or slow? I don't know.

Even though you tell me so

Words and ideas just don't flow.

Nothing done, nothing to show.

How do I know where I should go?

Where am I going? I don't know the way.

It isn't the future, it's living today.

Dealing with nonsense and trivial things.

The pressure, the urgent, frustration brings.

Minute by minute, hour to hour;

Losing control, having no power.

Where am I going? Please show me the way.

How can I manage to get through today?

Run

Run to keep your ticker goin'.

Run to keep your blood a-flowin'.

Run to keep your breath a-blowin'.

Run because you're never knowin'

What you might run into or

What you're runnin' from.

First Flight

(Author Anonymous)

Pity the poor babe left in the perch

With wings that were never undone.

Destined to die in his heart and his mind

The song that will never be sung.

But praise the brave child who stands on the edge,

Burning with desire to try.

Then, without warning, leaps into the wind

And suddenly learns how to fly.

[I found "First Flight" written on a piece of scratch paper and thumb tacked to the wall in a small hometown diner. I include here these two verses not knowing the author, but that they gave me the inspiration to write the next three verses, which I titled "Addendum."]

Addendum
{Inspired by First Flight}

But what of the child who never will fly

Due to no fault of his own.

Through some ill abuse or other excuse,

All life from his body is gone?

Left all alone, cast down to the depths

Of perpetual fear and despair.

Quite often dispatched, with guilt unattached,

To institutional care.

Born without wings, he closes his eyes

And soars, in his mind, to great height.

On heavenly winds he is lifted above,

In glorious, spiritual flight.

Work's The Thing

Dreams are things we throw away

After working hard each day

Just to keep the home fires burning

And the wheels of progress turning.

Dreamin's not the thing to do.

Unproductive ballyhoo.

Only makes the spirit soar.

Something else we can ignore.

Can the spirit pay the bills?

Work's the thing. Forget the frills.

Push the button, pull the string

We all know that work's the thing.

Crazy People

To review anew the times we blew.

Crazy people all are we.

Ask us not what is to be.

All we know is that we are

Shackled to a dying star.

We'll never pass this way again.

Who cares? We pass and trash and sin.

The Final Score

Do not think it's just a sport.

The game of life ends on His court.

How we serve, it matters not.

Double faults is all we've got.

It's our choice whom we shall serve.

The final judge prescribes our lot.

It doesn't count what points we score.

It's always LUV and nothing more.

The final score will matter more

When we're at Eternity's door.

US: LUV.　　　.HIM: LOVE

He comes to save us from above.

Tag

"You're it!" The children shout
And then all run about.
The "It" attempts to tag another,
"You're it!" is what they shout.

Jesus came and tagged me.
"Your mine." Is what He said.
I felt a new awakening,
As rising from the dead.

Now He said it's my turn
To go and tag another.
So off I went to tag one
That I could call my brother.

Some ran away so hard and fast,
Not wanting to get caught.
Not wanting to admit they knew
'Twas for their lives He bought.

With His own life He paid the price,
'Twas not a game He played.
He came with love and those He tagged
A Son of God He made.

Kick The Can
(a child's game)

Oh worm that I am – a sinful man
How can I be set free?
A children's game, but still the same
I hide behind a tree.

Satan comes to my hiding place
And says he's captured me.

My sins abound –I know I'm found
Lord have mercy on me.

Then the Spirit comes and kicks the can
And shouts, "Allee. Allee in free!"
"Allee, allee in free!"

For those He called to be set free
Predestined them to be.
Once again the Spirit sounds:
"Allee, allee in free!"

What Is Truth?

"What is truth?" Pilate said.

Although he didn't really care; instead

His interest lie in appeasing those

Who wanted this man dead.

They feared the truth, driven by their greed.

They demanded Pilate do the deed

They thought would save their high position;

The hypocrites chose of their own volition.

Only wanting this troubler to die.

And that is why they yelled,

"CRUCIFY! CRUCIFY!"

They got their way, so they thought.

Never knowing the sin they wrought

Only brought what the prophets taught.

That One should die to save the nation

So God could redeem His whole creation.

The Light Tonight

The light tonight is not so bright.

The darkness brings on fear and fright.

I need to keep my Lord in sight.

So that my life is His delight

And all I do is pure and right.

That I would love my God above

With all my heart, soul, mind and might.

Lord, make me humble, so I don't stumble.

Satan laughs, my faith to crumble.

LORD please take away my sin

And then forgive again,

Again.

In Church

That fellow sitting over there

Has a certain putrid air.

Smells like hell, ain't that sweet?

Who is this guy from off the street?

Would the ushers get a chair

And sit him in the corner there?

Oh my God! Had he farted?

That's what they thought as they departed.

They couldn't see he was scent to prove

They didn't care nor did they love

Some odorous one from God above.

He hadn't had a bath in weeks.

Those coming near would say he reeks.

They moved elsewhere not to care

For one who seeks to find somewhere

A friend, a home, a place to be

Cleaned up and then set free.

The Cost

Shackled pain

Has kept me bound

In darkness reign

No sight, no sound

Forever lost

In light I'm found

I count the cost

His life for mine.

The Blind Man

Lord, I've been blind all my life.

You asked what you could do for me.

Give me my sight and set me free

From this darkness and its grip on me.

He touched me and the light broke through.

Shattered the darkness and made me new.

He gave me a vision of His love and grace.

His blessing bestowed and my sin erase

The Aroma

It stinks. It's bunk.

Who'd read this junk?

More than a few,

Not knowing their pew,

Sit and smell

Of the stench of hell.

Evil swathed in pretty clothes

Not discerned by even those

Who sit in their own pew

With stuffed up nose.

I know, I know. I came from there.

I used to have an awful air

As I passed through every day.

But now I've found the better way.

He found me and He took my sin

And now I live my life in Him.

My Claim

In His name I claim

The victory

And overcame

What may today.

Step by step

I walk and talk

The path that's

Laid and paid.

To Him I know I owe

It all and call

On Him to guide and guard

Lest I should fall.

But even then and when

He comes to lift and gift

And save and pave

The way again.

So I may walk today

With Him.

Where Is The Light?

I look at the dark and speak to the void

How many times have I been annoyed

With the thought that I really don't know?

With the thought that I really don't know?

Where is my God? Where is He now?

When I speak with Him, do I really know how?

Is He here? Is He there? Does He really care

What I say, what I do as I sit in my pew?

Distraught with the thought of how little I count.

In His overall plan, I'm not much amount.

I pick and I choose, but I always lose.

The end will come and I'll pay my dues.

Dark is the night full of dread and of gloom.

Where is the light from the empty tomb?

They Who Sit and Wait

Even they who sit and wait

Serve the Lord.

For they take time to meditate

Upon His Word.

Their prayers are heard

By God above.

Who answers them

With perfect love.

Endlessly they rock in time

With perfect meter,

Perfect rhyme.

My Sin

I fear the judge who knows it all.

I fear the judge who since the fall,

Declared that death must pay for all

The sin that I have wallowed in.

Sins are gone; no longer taunt.

He's taken them from out the haunt

And tossed them farthest to the sea.

They can no longer bother me.

The Basin

I tell myself as I sit on the shelf,

I think it's my story. I think of my glory.

Of how I'll be used to hold all the gold

And not abused as I grow old.

He filled me with water to wash other's feet,

To take off the grime and the dirt from the street.

Now I'm back on the shelf, He finished His task.

Please, use me for great things is all I ask.

About My Art

Just another picture? – NO!

But to you it may seem so.

To me it came from deep within

Where Christ resides – and no more sin

Controls my life, but only He

Who lives in me.

The One who died to set me free.

Lord I pray that all I do

Will be used to honor you.

Morning Fog

Morning fog obscures all vision beyond a few hundred feet.

Dozens of small sparrows flit and dance among the branches.

Without their questioning, He has provided their sustenance

and purpose.

Mental fog obscures understanding of why I exist.

He has set me here to glorify Him.

Though I am small and unworthy

All I need is to trust and obey.

His grace is sufficient.

"When I consider Your heavens, the work of Your fingers, The moon and the stars, which You have ordained, What is man that You are mindful of him, And the son of man that you visit him?"

Psalm 8:3-4

Just Do It!

Lord, what would You have me do?

Where would You have me go?

How can I serve You Lord?

I really need to know.

"Just do it! Just do it!

And as you go through it

Just look everywhere

And you'll see that I'm there."

"God on high, hear my prayer.

In my need, You have always been there.

Bring me home.

Bring me home.

Bring me home.

Bring me home."

- Les Miserables

Look At Me

Visitors sitting next to me.

I will show them how to be.

I'll put my hands up in the air,

Then they'll know I really care.

If I sing out really loud

To show them I'm above the crowd.

I'll sway and move and even dance.

They'll think I'm in a spiritual trance.

Shout "Amen" or "Preach it, brother."

They will know I'm like no other.

They will look and then they'll see

How God's blessings fall on me.

A big, black Bible in my hand,

With pages marked, they'll think that's grand.

That should draw them to the Lord

And I won't have to say a word.

"Blind guides," He said to them, not me.

Because I've done it right, you see.

Look at me, look at me.

I'm the one that you should see.

I have Kool-Aid here to drink;

Sweet and tasty, makes you think.

Drink it long, drink it slow.

Guaranteed to make you grow

To be successful, just like me.

That is what you ought to be.

Adam's Cry

Where art Thou, O Lord?

Where art Thou, my Light?

The darkness is dark,

As black as the night.

Christlike humility

Love for my enemy

Are not in me.

All hinder me

From knowing Him

As I should be.

I am not free,

But slave to sin

Till He comes in

And sets me free.

Free to be a slave to Him

In joyful community

With God and man

As created be.

I Saw Him

I saw him. I saw him.

A horrible sight.

I saw him. I saw him.

The angel of light.

He taunts me and haunts me

Tho' I put up a fight.

He laughs at my efforts

And then blinds my sight.

I turn to my Lord

And trust that He's there.

He promised to stay,

He promised to care.

He is here. He is here.

There is no more to fear.

His presence has caused

The air to be clear.

He fills my heart

When ere He comes near.

And the rest of the world

Will all disappear.

What Is The Point?

What is the point of all this stuff?

I can never do enough.

My God, my God, I just don't know

What to do? Where to go?

Oh my God help me to say

The words you want. That's what I pray.

One goes down, the other up.

If you're willing, share my cup.

I stayed and played it like a game

Until He came and I felt shame.

His call was all I needed then

To deal with sin, I'm born again.

And now I know the way to go

To follow Him and I will grow.

I've Always Known

In my life I've always known

That which You have always shown.

Though there are times I failed to see

The path that You had set for me.

You called, I came, You set me free

To be what I am called to be.

Lord that I would live for you

In all I am and all I do.

A friend, a son, an heir of love,

A blessing from my GOD above.

The Prodigal Son

Wide is the gate and broad is the way

I think that I shall go this day.

Looks great. 'Twill most productive be.

An easy way, as I can see.

I want to grow in wealth and fame

And everyone will know my name.

Give me my share and I'll be gone.

Out of your hair. No more your son.

I smell the air, a fragrance fair

That I'll not share with anyone.

Specks And Planks

Tho' my eyes are full of planks and beams

I still see specks in other's dreams.

Please help me Lord to see that I

Must remove the plank from my eye

To help my brother clean his eye

Of all the specks that I should spy.

His needs are great, as I draw near

What I should do is not that clear.

I know he needs to know you Lord.

What I must do is share your Word.

Tho' true, his faults I should not find

Until I know what's in your mind.

To deal with this inhuman place

Would hide from him your loving grace.

He Is Near

Most of our lives we drink from the sewers of this world rather than ask of Him who will freely give us living water.

"a fountain of water springing up into everlasting life."

The people prostitute themselves before the idols of the world. They bring the wrath of God upon themselves and upon their neighbors.

I know my redeemer lives. I know that I've been redeemed.

No reason to be filled with fear even though my death is near.

I know that He is here.

Worthless

I know I am worthless as I sit in this chair

Wondering and hoping that You will be there.

To choose me and use me to show that You care.

Have mercy on me. This is my prayer.

I watched the games and saw them excel.

I know I am worthless and going to hell.

Unless You should come and take me away

And change my heart, that's what I pray.

To give me Your Spirit and cleanse me anew.

Be with me Lord in all that I do.

God's Plan

Where am I in God's plan?

Am I elect or do I stand

Condemned?

He said He'd come to call me friend,

To wash me clean; forgive my sin.

continued

I read His law. I've broken all.

Guilty, guilty. Since the fall.

I know I must in Him I trust

To take away this sinful lust

That's kept me bound to Satan's will

Whose sole desire is to kill

The grace I've found through Calvary's hill.

One forever with the life and love

Brought to us from God above.

An Ungodly Life

Most do not know and really don't care.

They all have their lives and burdens to bear.

They have not heard God's Holy Word.

Nor listened to one who is trying to share

The knowledge and love he received from above.

Caught up in their sin of the darkness and night,

You think they would win if they'd stand up and fight.

Their efforts are poor, they can't do much more.

If they'd only listen and open the door.

A door to new life away from the strife.

Away from the sin of an ungodly life.

I Came To The Garden

I came to the garden to meditate.

I came to the garden, but found I was late.

They already had taken my Savior away.

Where they had gone, I couldn't say.

Later I found the cross was the way

Where they had killed Him, my sin to pay.

They said they had seen Him after that day.

Perhaps it was just a game that they play.

My trust is in Him and not what they say.

All I can do is trust and obey.

I did not see Him; all I can do

Is trust in the Word He gave me and you.

Gone is the darkness, the dread and the gloom.

Bright is the light from the empty tomb.

Oh to be with Him on His return.

Not with the goats who surely will burn.

Come Holy Spirit and work from within.

Come Holy Spirit and deal with my sin.

THOUGHTS
from the
PEW

Paul "Herb" Frazier

Thoughts From The Pew

"*Herb's poetry has a way of unmasking the superficial -
in the world and in us - while reminding us we were
made for so much more.*"

Rev. Raymond W. Cameron, Jr.
First Presbyterian Church (ARP)
Lake Placid, Florida

Introduction to Book 7

On October 21, 2011, God said to me: "Give me the time and I will give you the words and pictures." He has been faithful.

"THOUGHTS FROM THE PEW" was originally published in 2013 and is an accumulation of poems I wrote prior to 2013. I present these simple writings to the glory of God and to His Son, Jesus Christ, that with His Spirit they may be used to His purpose.

"Thought provoking words, sometimes humorous and sarcastic, leaving the reader to contemplate his own (spiritual development) position in this scheme called life." phf - HS

Soli Deo Gloria

I Gotta' Go
(The Prodigal Son)

"Dad, I gotta' git, I gotta' go."
"Son, tell me where is it that you want to go?"
"I gotta' go to a place far away,
A place to have fun, a place I can play.
A place far away from my Dad and my bro'.
I gotta' git, I gotta 'go.
Give me my money and I will split.
I gotta' go, I gotta' git."

Packed up and goin' someplace to have fun.
"Come on and join me. I got the 'mon'."

"This is wonderful, this is great.
Back workin' the farm, that's what I hate.
Runnin' with women and drinkin' this wine.
Ever'thin's wonderful, ever'thin's fine."

Meanwhile a famine has taken it's toll.
Can't think on that now, 'cause I'm on a roll.

Hmph! Looked in my purse, cash gettin' low.
Gotta' watch spendin', gotta' go slow.
Can't pay the bills, - no party tonight.
Maybe my friends will help in my plight.

Ever'ones gone. Where did they go?
Now that I'm broke, with nothin' to show.
I'll get a job and make some more dough.
That's what I'll do, that's where I'll go.

Can't find work, 'cept pigs to feed.
Not the kind of job that I need.

I gotta' go. I've had enough.
Livin' with pigs an' eatin' their stuff.
Maybe my Dad will hire me to work,
After I tell Him that I've been a jerk.
I'll make a new life on my father's farm.
Perhaps he will let me, without any harm.

Here comes my Dad. He's runnin' to meet me.
After what I've done, how can he greet me
With a kiss and a hug? Why don't he beat me?

A party for me? That's what he had.
How could he do this when I've been so bad?

Unlimited grace he's showered on me.
Now I'm forgiven and now truly free.

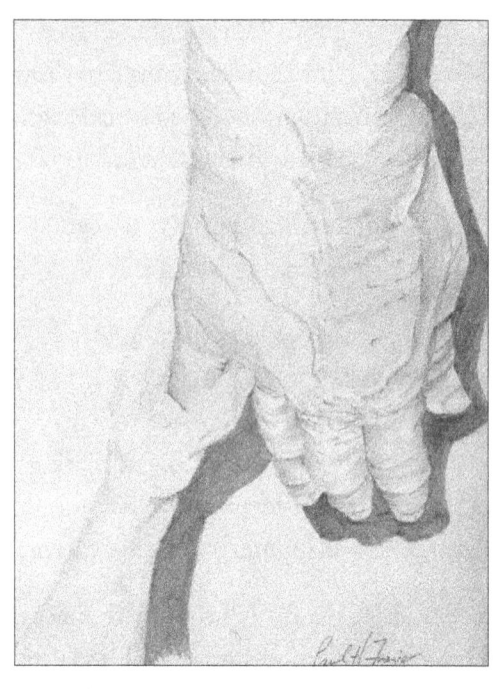

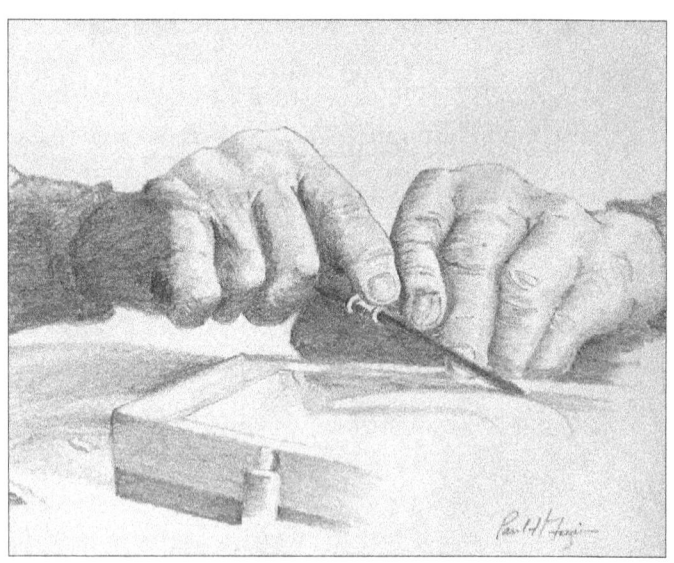

Hands

Hands tell it all
Of the skill and the call.
The work that shows
Trials and woes.

They mold a life
Where'er it goes.
And tells a story
To all of those
Who see the scars
From painful blows.
With sweat and blood
From hateful foes.

He only knows
From where strength flows.
On whom the life He bestows.
Lift up your hands and show
The wear and tear
From years and tears
Of loving care.

Tonight a bright and shining light
Show hands engaging in the fight.
Nailed to a cross to give us sight
That we might live eternally.

Three Groups

There are three groups of people.

1. Those who truly know their GOD and follow His Word.

   They will experience the cool refreshing heir-conditioning of heaven.

2. Those who claim to know God but follow the ways of the world.

   They will feel the heat from standing too close to the fire.

3. Those who reject God.

They are toast.

The Aroma of Sin

I smell, I stink. This I knew.

Before I ever sat in this pew.

Here in the church, my sin in full view.

Those around me moved away.

I offended them, they seemed to say.

I needed someone to help me to see,

That I could be clean; that I could be free.

No one came. They all moved away.

I guess I'll leave, still stinking this day.

What's Not Important

A note not played

No picture displayed

A flower decayed

A silent parade

Of life's charade.

No choices made

A future dismayed.

All we've got

Is a burial plot

To show what's not

Important.

Dark is the night

Full of dread and of gloom.

Where is the light

From the empty tomb?

All At Peace

I sit in the dark

The only sound: a clock ticking.

Measuring time quickly gone.

In the distance, a light

Reflecting on the still water.

All is quiet, all at peace.

Except my soul.

"Oh my soul. Why are you so disquieted within me?"

Psalm 43:5

Homeless

A homeless child of the night,

His life a horrible plight.

Afraid of the dark,

Would hide in the park,

Waiting for morning's bright light.

A homeless child of the street,

Would steal in order to eat.

Although he was there

The world didn't care

Someone they don't want to meet.

Reflections

Looking west across the lake,

The sun sets behind our house.

If there are no clouds interrupting the rays,

It splashes brilliant colors across the blue,

And they reflect on the placid water.

Sometimes so bright, the glare

Forces us to pull the shades, blocking the view.

Then the darkness comes and engulfs our lake.

Often when I rise early I am rewarded

With the setting moon

Dancing it's reflection on the water.

And I thank God for His blessings.

Living Sounds

Rambling rhetoric
Hollow sounds
The scream of endless silence
Forgotten promises
Broken vows
Dead dreams
Unquenched thirst
The thundering noise of crashing souls

Enter One

Patching pieces

Healing wounds

Lifting up

Born anew

Quietly

Loving

Guiding

Providing

Whispering softly

"Eternal Life"

A Boat Named Fear

I heard the call, but I said "No."

So much to do, places to go.

I wished for time, but can't say, "Whoa."

To stop the clock. To take it slow.

Flying by so ever fast

Before you know it time has passed.

And then its gone,

With what to show?

No time to love,

No time to grow.

I heard the call,

But built a wall

Strong and tall

That wouldn't fall.

And when He called again this year,

I couldn't hear.

And stayed within a boat named fear.

The Message

I've spent my life saying why don't they

Do this, or that, or the other?

When I share they don't care

So I say, "Why bother?"

When we pray, in what we say,

We must try to discover

What He wants or what He wills:

The message from the Lover.

Every day I need to pray,

"What is His will for me?"

That I might give and truly live

To be what I should be.

The Mainstream Church

Motivational pump, materialist dump,

Impressive sales, quality fails.

The profits soar as we want more.

Parking lots filled with expensive cars,

The numbers say success is ours.

The church shall reign forevermore.

A Mercedes parked by the entrance door

Is proof that blessings come to those

Who wear the right designer clothes.

Mainstreet Media

Gone are the roots that cling to the sands of time

Barely a reef to protect the shore

Waves tossing plastic and petroleum

Lives twisted amongst worldly debris

Discarded through the outfalls of progress.

Purification by dissemination has become humanities'

pollution.

Lust for self-gratification has become the diseased leaven

Infecting the loaf on which the media feeds us day by day.

Caring not about the poisonous death awaiting those

Who partake of the proffered garbage.

What's The Rush?

Each morning I rise to the sounds of heavy metal.

A cacophony of clanging symbols and sounding brass.

I mount my chariot and enter the morning maze;

Driven by the pursuit of pleasure and self-gratification.

Juggling time and passion in a downward spiral of

self-addiction.

I cling to the sin and scream at the void.

Eternity traded for a moment's rush.

Caught up in the daily race,

Urgent and demanding pace.

Extracting life from all who run.

Unfocused eyes that cannot see

Rising dead or burning tree.

Blinded to the truthful One.

And now I wonder if He'll come — again.

Testimony

I stopped at a light

And looked to my right.

He came out of the bushes.

Oh no! - What a sight.

I know he must have spent the night

Under a willow,

A rock for a pillow;

Instead of a bed,

Slept on rushes.

Dirty and sloppy he gave us a fright.

I know it's not funny

He needed some money.

As he approached I drove out of sight.

It could have been my Lord I left

Standing on the corner.

I went back, retraced my track,

To see if he was there.

I know I did the right thing

To show I didn't care.

For Me or Not For Me
(That is the question)

It has to be all for me.

If it's not, let it rot.

I don't care what you've got.

I've invested quite a lot.

From what I've sold

I want my gold,

To enjoy before I'm old.

The Sacrifice of Living

Loosen the bands that hinder life;

The only thing worth living.

Though this world be filled with strife,

'Tis God's own son in giving

His life for ours, then ours to Him,

The sacrifice of living.

I stand in awe that He should come

For a worthless one like me.

He gave Himself to become my sin

When they nailed Him to the tree.

Listening To The Preacher Preach

While listening to the preacher preach;

The man in front of me, fast asleep

While listening to the preacher preach

How I'm to love and I'm to teach

Of many things beyond my reach.

The young girl in the third row seat –

WOW – Stop. Deny the flesh I must.

Forgive me Lord, I do beseech,

That I should lust

While listening to the preacher preach.

There's that guy full of pride,

Probably thinks the Savior died

Just for him.

And the woman in that hat.

Imagine that. If she sat

In front of me I couldn't see

continued

While listening to the preacher preach.

Music's loud for such a crowd.

Raising hands – Is that allowed?

What's that roar? Did someone score?

Or did he snore? That man asleep in front of me

While listening to the preacher preach.

It's her fault – immodesty

To dress like that for all to see.

You can't blame me.

What? Pluck out my eye?

That's absurd. Is that the Word?

He makes me try to see

That this is my depravity.

Forgive me Lord, I do beseech

While listening to the preacher preach.

What did he say?

That I must pay?

Well – anyway later today

The word I heard I must critique.

While listening to the preacher preach.

What Do You See?

What do you see when you look at a tree?

Do you see the root? How deep it goes?

Do you see the fruit and how it grows?

Do you see the sap, the way it flows?

What do you see when you look at the sky?

Sunrise? Sunset? Glaring bright?

Windswept clouds? Unmeasured height?

Twinkling darkness? Moonlit night?

What do you see when you look at me?

Do you see roots or branches and fruit?

Storm clouds, rainbows or sun?

How I grow and where I go?

Or in me do you see – His Son?

It Hurts

Pain expands and tightens its relentless grip,

Until no other reality exists.

Her eyes looked up at me and said,

"Daddy, it hurts."

In my helplessness I cried.

In my trials I looked up to God and cried,

"Daddy, it hurts."

He came to me and said,

"For you I died."

Oh Lord

Oh Lord there must be something wrong,

It seems that when I've gone this long

Without a word I've heard from you.

I do not know what I'm to do.

I'm sure that I am not so pure.

Nor that I can always endure

The threats and jabs that come from him

That wants to lead me into sin.

I always pray that I won't fall

And that I'll hear you when you call.

Sometimes it's tough and life gets rough

And I don't seem to do enough.

Although I know you 've done it all.

If in my pride I should stumble,

Lift me up and make me humble.

In fear and shame I come disgraced.

continued

You died for me; my sin erased.

Yet even when in sin I go,

Yes Lord, I know, you love me so.

Teach me your Word that I may grow.

Then, through my life, help me to show

Your love so others come to know

The truth you died for them also.

It's from above, your love and grace

Has come to bring me to the place

Where I will see you face to face

And there abide in your embrace.

Do It My Way

Why doesn't God do it my way?

You think He'd let me have a say.

At least ask me for my advice.

To help Him out, that would be nice.

Advising Him is what I do.

Critiquing others from the pew.

I'm always ready with a word or two

To tell His saints what they should do.

Why doesn't God do it my way?

I'm sure I'd have more time to play.

Life Bounteous

I don't always understand the plan He has for me.

As I walk and talk (too much) the path isn't clear to see.

Although the light is very bright, I think the problem is
with my sight.

I always dread to look ahead, knowing someday
I'll be dead.

Lord, is it true when I'm with you that there will
only be a few

Who saw the way you came that day

And know the cost you had to pay?

I took a look at your book and former paradigms
were shook.

Reading your Word, your voice I heard.

Now I know I've been assured.

Sin abhorred, in one accord; seeking you and your reward.

In all the earth there is no mirth.

Only that which has no worth.

I conclude we must exclude a life that's crude and
death elude.

I now proclaim, in His name, no more shame,
because He came.

Not to discuss or make a fuss, though the world is
contemptuous.

He offers us life bounteous – in Him.

Alone With My Thoughts

Alone with my thoughts, I turned to God.

He breathed His Spirit into this clod.

What then will He do with this clump of sod?

All night long my dreams a haunt.

All day long my sins a taunt.

What do you do with a dirty old shoe;

Worn and torn and covered with doo?

Why do I feel my life is a waste?

I tried everything that I could taste.

I tried and cried deep inside, then I died.

No place to hide. To myself I had lied.

When I die will I be in a place where I'm free

From the haunts and the taunts

That all trouble me?

Will I go to a place with my sins all erased?

Or will I suffer for that which I did?

That which I've done and cannot be hid

From the One who had made me and bade me to come?

Come home to Him and to live as His son.

All My Thoughts

All my thoughts go everywhere

Down to earth and in the air.

Some would say that I don't care,

But that's not fair.

I want to think on something sure,

Something good, something pure.

My mind is racing, screaming by.

I try to focus, really try.

Things come creeping on the sly,

Worldly distractions catch my eye.

To clear my mind is what I ought,

To focus on a single thought.

Lord I try to take the time

To find the words to make life rhyme.

Perhaps my heart is not aright

To fast and pray throughout the night

I hope will help to set my sight

On something good, on something right.